51
RULES FOR THE PERFECT GENTLEMAN

SENYO M. ADJABENG

Lumière Creatif

Research and editorial assistance:
Role Model Africa

Email:
Info@rolemodelafrica.org
Rolemodelafrica@gmail.com

Website:
www.rolemodelafrica.org

Telephone:
+233-248-417-088

TABEL OF CONTENT

DEDICATION

This book is dedicated to my father Justice (Rtd.) E. D. K. Adjabeng, a retired Justice of the Supreme Court of the Republic of Ghana, and my Twin Sister, Senna.

ACKNOWLEDGEMENT

This work is a product of a few months of isolation in 'the wilderness' where my deeper-most part of being came to life.

For the development and production of this book, I am eternally grateful to:
My amazing wife, Harriet, for sticking with me.
To my parents, who, in more ways than one, showed me the pathway to a principled life.

My circle of friends; Godwin D, Kweku Aaron, the wonderful business networking group and family known as The 'Senators', 'TAC5 Women of Substance'…all of who continue to give me great encouragement, support and strength in my work life.

I have stated in this book the Four Way Test of Rotary. I thank and acknowledge Rotary International and toast to all Rotarians wherever they may be.
Finally, to Apostle Dr. Aaron Ami-Narh, (President of the Apostolic Church, Ghana), and his wife, 'Mummy Joe' who have been a strong primatial pillar of direction and spiritual focus.

INSPIRED BY:

The Gentleman's Rule Book…according to Justice (Rtd.) E. D. K. Adjabeng

DISCLAIMER:

The entire content of this book is strictly produced as a guide and subject to readers' choice of interpretation and application. Content does not constitute commands or instructions for strict adherence, but a guide for life and the readers' informed decision making.

PREFACE

My father is my greatest inspiration. I grew up knowing there is a rule or law to everything, including why there is a ceiling over a person's head and why people have to sleep on a 'bedding' and not the bare floor, why they have to wear particular clothing, and why footwear should have a certain look and feel. I grew up appreciating the fact that there is a structure to everything, and with each structure, its own rules.

Society is constructed on these rules. Successful people are often those who have studied, understood, lived and played by these rules. Everyone is called upon to know and live by the rules of life and living it in one way or the other. Playing by the rules puts one at an advantage over the other person. And yet, not playing by the rules means being played by others to one's detriment.

The rules of life, especially in a 'male dominated world,' are not composed in one book or culture or language. However, the basic rules for survival and being an outstanding man can be summarised and shared for the good of all. That is what this book seeks to achieve.

To be a man, a gentleman, who stands out of the lot in a very competitive world, it is important to know about the basic things that make a man great. This book provides a window into this world of knowledge. By reading this book, I do hope eyes will open, lives will be touched and will be positively transformed. That, men will become better human beings seeking to show kindness to all, and to love and provide for others in need and in any small way possible.

Who is a perfect gentleman?

John Bridges, in his book, *How to be a Gentleman*, states that being a gentleman "means thinking of others, being there when needed, and knowing when you are not needed."

A chivalrous, courteous, gallant and honorable man, who is committed to creating value and making a difference in the lives of all around him, may pass as a perfect gentleman. But, what and by whose standards do we determine the perfection of a gentleman? Man is certainly not perfect. There is a residue of inherent evil in every man.

However, the concept of a perfect gentleman is an ideal state, a moral height that every man should seek to attain. This book should serve as a guide for coaching younger men and mentoring adult developing men to become outstanding perfect gentlemen.

Becoming perfect gentlemen in every aspect of their social and spiritual lives, drawing a work-life balance and also exuding positive vibes towards the mysteries and philosophies of Life and Afterlife, should not be overlooked.

51 rules of the perfect gentleman highlights some morals that most men usually do not consider to have any negative impact, when they are ignored.

PART 1:

THE ESSENCE OF LIFE

"There are only two forces in the world, the Sword and the Spirit. In the long run, the Sword will always be conquered by the Spirit."

~Napoleon Bonaparte~

RULE #1

Life and Living it

There is more to life than food, shelter and clothes. It is important to find true satisfaction and contentment which often comes from being true to ones' self.
~ Senyo M. Adjabeng

. . . .

Self-deception and disillusion are a canker that send many to self-destruction. When a person lives a lie continuously, it comes to a point where life itself becomes a lie and an illusion. A gentleman leads his life in confidence knowing what he wants, what he wants to do with his life at any point in time and what his expectations of himself and others are.

A life well-lived is not one that has no regrets, but one that is satisfying, knowing that even failures have been well-utilized for a certain positive purpose.

I have often asked myself what the last thoughts of a dying man are. In the end, and when the certainty of death draws near, what inner feeling dominates a man's psyche? Contentment? Fear? Or a humbling confidence that after all is said and done, and on a balance of probabilities, it is 'well done'?

Life and living it is what a man makes of life itself - opportunities, challenges and successes all put together in a swelling pot of judgement. There is so much in today's world that is orchestrated to derail a focused, healthy, peace-loving and a clear-minded lifestyle.

A wise man advised me in my younger days not to lead a life that makes me look over my shoulder at any point of my life-long journey. A perfect gentleman is one who can say at any point in time that even with some regrets, there is a general joy to have so far lived a life to be proud of, and which has been worth living.

RULE #2

Belief and Spirituality

"The light always conquers the darkness! This is simply science."
~ Senyo M. Adjabeng

....

A gentleman must and will always believe in something. Beyond the physical, there is the spiritual which will always attract man's attention.

The awes of earthly happenings will drive a man to look for answers beyond the physical. Whether for the forces of darkness or light, a Perfect Gentleman must carefully choose where he belongs.

RULE #3

Religion

"Religion goes a long way to determine a man's fate."
~ Senyo M. Adjabeng

. . . .

Religion guides and defines a man's focus in dealing with the unknown beyond the physical. There are many things a man will struggle to believe. In the quest to search for the truths of the unknown, a man will come across many beliefs, religions, philosophies and opinions.

The search for truth of things generally unknown is critical. However, the recognition of what is truth is determined by many factors. A perfect gentleman is one who finds a balance between what is generally acceptable as truth and what, in his personal conviction, is truth.

The decision to choose and belong to a religion or otherwise is a choice - a choice so critical that a man becomes shaped, clothed and embodied by the religion he chooses or otherwise.

A perfect gentleman does not flirt with religion, but chooses a specific religion and commits to it devotedly. On the contrary, a man who chooses not to believe in and belong to any religion must find an alternative truth in the things of the unknown - a quest which could be vain.

RULE #4

Principles and Philosophy

"Principles Make a Man. And as for Philosophy, a man's opinion is certainly non-negotiable.
~ Senyo M. Adjabeng

....

Principles define who a man is today or will become tomorrow. Of the many things that determine identity, a man's principles are one of the most outstanding factors that defines a man's unique identity - as in who he truly is.

A man's philosophy is his unique thoughts and reasoning regarding life in general and all other subject matter within the spheres of life. For example, each man has and should necessarily have an opinion on History, Politics, War, Religion, Success, Death, Eternity etc.

Principles are derived from a person's unique philosophy and are the set of truths, propositions, codes, concepts, ideas, ground rules and theories that serve as a foundation for how a man lives, behaves and reasons. A man's principles direct the paths he takes, the choices he makes and the dreams he pursues.

A Perfect Gentleman is one with clear, unambiguous and outstanding principles.

RULE #5

Money and Wealth

Money is but a commodity, but true wealth is in the heart of man.
~ Senyo M. Adjabeng

....

Money is a medium of exchange, and its acquisition in volumes may not mean much. What is done and achieved with the money so accumulated is what brings value to it. The essence of life should be for the betterment of society and the alleviation of suffering aggravated by poverty, disease, lack of knowledge and mental bankruptcy.

Wealth constitutes the attainment of affluence, riches, treasures, assets etc. A truly wealthy man, however, is one who is remembered many centuries after death for deeds that go beyond the accumulation of riches, assets and property. The conversion of riches, property and affluence into value for fellow humans, friends and family, neighbours and all citizens of the world constitutes true wealth.

True wealth is in the heart of man. The deeds of man, through the resources at his disposal and under his control, may make him truly wealthy or otherwise. In life, it does not matter how much riches and treasures one accumulates; what matters is what a person is remembered by, long after they are gone. The footprint a gentleman leaves in the sands of time is what makes him a truly wealthy gentleman.

RULE #6

Rest and Leisure

Rest is biologically good and essentially mandatory for the nourishment of body, mind and soul. As for leisure, it breeds hope, and engenders focus and the tranquility of mind.

....

Pope Francis said "together with a culture of work, there must be a culture of leisure as gratification. To put it another way: people who work must take time to relax, to be with their families, to enjoy themselves, read, listen to music, play a sport."

The quality of a person's life, in terms of health, is largely impacted by how much rest and leisure they enjoy. And, while engaging in rest and leisure, on many occasions, a gentleman interacts with others and benefits from the blessings of social networking.

As Santiago says in Paulo Coelho's 'The Alchemist'; **"sometimes, it's better to be with the sheep, who don't say anything."** Silence and some peace and quiet are necessary ingredients for quality life. Leisure liberates the mind and frees the spirit.

A perfect gentleman must have a careful balance between hard work and rest and leisure.

RULE #7

Travel

Once a year, a gentleman should go someplace they have never been before.

....

Traveling is an adventure every man owes to himself. It is the only thing, when purchased, makes one richer. The arts of learning about other lands and cultures lies in travel. As a man does this, he tends to understand his own culture and sense of being much more.

Traveling is experiential; it arouses feelings deeper than one can express. Some have proclaimed that travel tends to turn a man into a story teller. There's everything to gain in travel and nothing to gain in staying put. Travel is like reading a book; until one immerses him or herself in it, one cannot really find the value in it.

A perfect gentleman must travel and see the world to become richer in thought and deed. For when the body is old and frail, there can be no excuse for staying put all the days of one's life.

RULE #8

Women, Children and Family

A woman compliments a man. A child brings joy to the home. Family brings strength to the soul, nourishing the spirit with 'oil'.
~ Senyo M. Adjabeng

. . . .

There is no replacement for family - family defines a man. Family is the only possession a man can truly claim without cost or conscience. That said, there will always be one special woman in a man's life.

As proclaimed by Margaret Thatcher, **"if you want something said, ask a man; if you want something done, ask a woman."** A woman completes a man, and often assists him to achieve his destiny or otherwise. A woman is inspiration to a male soul, and drives performance or otherwise in all aspects of his endeavours.

A gentleman should aspire to meet and share his life with a woman. If a child is born out of the union, it surely is a blessing and source of joy. Above all, a gentleman should surround himself with some female advisors as an intuitive compliment to the male egoistic 'macho'.

RULE #9

Sex

Sex, and a lot of it, is good for man. By all means, a man should get good, safe and quality sex as frequently as possible. But alas, the pursuit of same has been the doom of many men.

According to experts, Sex boosts and helps keep the immune system working effectively, boosts libido, improves bladder performance, controls and lowers blood pressure, counts as exercise and burning of calories, lowers the risk of heart attack, lessens pain and may make prostate cancer less likely.

From extensive research findings, sex is yet to be proven as harmful to man, except in cases where medical conditions require abstinence from and reduced or controlled sexual activity. In essence, sex as in good, safe sex, improves wellbeing.

A perfect gentleman is one who strives to master the act and art of granting sexual pleasure. Doing it is not enough as doing it well. Sex, as in love making, is a unique emotional communication between two special souls. A perfect gentleman, during sex, should not only be concerned about his satisfaction, but must ensure his partner enjoys every moment of it. He can always ask questions on what tickles her fancy. Sex is a privilege, and must be accorded same.

RULE #10

Success

Each man defines his own objectives of life, the extent of achievement and defines his own destiny. Success is what a man says it is.

. . . .

A man is successful when he has achieved, to a large extent, the objectives of life he set for himself. The extent to which a man achieves his dreams makes him successful or otherwise. The race of life is often against oneself, and not third persons.

To the world, success is the 'accomplishment of an aim or purpose,' and the 'favourable outcome' of a venture, scheme or undertaking often set by society and community. To some, success is riches, academic or career heights of achievement and accomplishment. This generalisation of what success is, however, may be fictional.

What defines true success is the inner joy and contentment of self-achievement. In essence, a man can never be successful when he plays by the rules of society and community, for no man has ever been successful in meeting the expectations of others, society and community.

A true and perfect gentleman sets standards and objectives in every aspect of his life, and strives to attain them. The extent of such attainment reflects and defines success. Success is the true inner feeling of contentment and accomplishment.

PART 2:
GROOMING

"Simplicity, good taste and grooming are the three fundamentals of good dressing and these do not cost money"

~ Christian Dior ~

RULE #11

Hair and Skin Care

A well-groomed hair and well-maintained skin represent image, poise and trendiness. It reflects living with the 'times' and projects a confident stature.

....

Daymond John said that **"good grooming is integral, and impeccable style is a must. If you don't look the part, no one will want to give you time or money"**. It has also been said that 'what you see is what you get'.

Appearance opens the strangest of doors. How a man looks begins from the skin and hair. A perfect combination of style, identity and health care must be factors a gentleman should consider for grooming decisions on hair and skin care.

Cleanliness is Godly. A major factor for managing hair should be for cleanliness foremost, and then looks. A younger fresher look is always more receptive than a bushy unkempt look. Depending on a person's trade and profession, hair style should be an important consideration in any decision for hair grooming.

The choice to keep facial hair or otherwise should be to improve one's looks. A gentleman may try several looks involving facial hair or no facial hair, to determine the best look. A decision to keep facial hair must be accompanied by the commitment to constantly cater for it - cutting, trimming, shaping, waxing etc.

Some cultures keep and retain substantial amounts of pubic hair. However, keeping pubic hair poses health risks and increases chances of catching skin and other infections. Hence, a decision to keep pubic hair must be accompanied by an absolute mentality and responsibility of cleanliness - washing, disinfecting, airing etc. A gentleman's rule, however, is to keep little or no pubic hair, if one can help it.

Knowing one's skin type, whether oily or dry, helps in skin care decision-making. Natural skin care products, (products with natural plant and food extracts), are more encouraged, as they contain limited amounts of artificial ingredients that may have side effects on the skin and body. Men with oily skin may use 'drier' skin care products, (natural), while men with dry skin types may use oilier skin care products designed for men.

The irony of 'skin care and toning' is that light skinned persons seek to 'tone' by darkening the skin through methods such as sun-bathing, while dark skinned persons seek to 'tone' their skin by lightening the skin color through various forms of bleaching. A gentleman's rule for skin care should be to improve skin health, rather than to change skin color.

Tattoos have become synonymous with skin care as related to body art. A gentleman's rule is to remember that tattoos cost more to remove than to apply. They remain on the skin forever as the skin ages with time. When deciding to have a tattoo, a gentleman should answer the question; 'how will this look 30 years from now?'

Renee Rouleau admonishes: **"be good to your skin. You'll wear it every day for the rest of your life.**

RULE #12

Massage

Until a man gets a first massage, the magical effect of massage, in his opinion, will remain 'a myth of pampered comfort for the rich'.
~ Senyo M. Adjabeng

. . . .

Studies in a growing body of research have shown and continue to verify the efficacy of massage therapy for health and wellness. Research has shown that administered over six weeks, massage therapy is able to significantly 'reduce pain, fatigue and spasticity in patients with multiple sclerosis'. Massage therapy is also known to help in the management of anxiety, digestive disorders, headaches, insomnia and related stress, myofascial pain syndrome, soft tissue strains and sports injury.

Massage is also known to help manage mental health issues such as depression, neurotransmitter and hormonal imbalance, blood pressure and circulatory issues, as well as work- related stress in health care and other professionals.

The shorter-term benefits of massage, however, is as magical as the immediate relaxation and relief a good massage offers a person. Massage is known to improve sleep disorders and enhance relaxation and rest. Massage improves the body's immunity to disease. Above all, research has now proven that massage does not only speed up recovery in injuries such as sports injury, but that massage therapy actually has a 'healing effect'.

The effect of massage is in the power of touch, and apart from receiving good doses of massage, a gentleman should learn to incorporate touch into his daily routine. Holding hands, hugging, cuddling and self-massage and other touch-related activity confirms the capacity of a gentleman to love and be loved.

RULE #13

Nail Care

Nails and feet say a lot about a man. It's been said that 'don't let anyone with bad nails tell you how to live your life. Clean and well-groomed nails are a must for the perfect gentleman

. . . .

"Your hands and feet never take a day off so take care of them" says Tammy Tailor.

Apart from health reasons, there is every reason to take good care of nails as a man. Research has shown that 80% of communicable diseases are transmitted by touch. Again, experts say that without a vaccine, 'one of the single most important things you can do to prevent getting the flu is to wash your hands'. Hand wash is not that effective with long, dirty fingernails, as dirt trapped in overgrown fingernails is difficult to dislodge.

Nail care, to many a man, is considered an unnecessary comfort or a semblance of gay/homosexual behavior. However, research shows that many men are paying more attention to grooming, including nail/cuticle care. Research shows that the male grooming industry is drastically changing, with men spending on male specific toiletries, instead of spending on only shaving products.

According to the Independent, (UK), world market estimates for men's toiletries topped a whopping 14.8 billion pounds in 2016, growing averagely year on year at 20% per annum from 2010. The growing trend is that men are beginning to pay more attention to their looks today than their predecessors. Male grooming and nail care is not an exclusive behavior for gay/homosexuals only, but for all professional men.

First impressions are everything. According to mensfitness.com, **"if you are a businessman, grimy paws aren't a great reflection on your professionalism… Your hands are on display. Men and Women don't want to shake a claw or stare at filthy fingernails."**

A gentleman's rule is to keep short clean nails at all times. This should not cost money if one learns to do it himself. A good pair of nail care tools should do the trick. Nails do not need to be polished, even though colorless nail polish gives nails an enhanced natural look.

RULE #14

Underwear

A man is what he wears underneath his clothing. Clean trendy underwear most often exudes self-confidence and a sense of true manhood. A perfect gentleman should keep at least a dozen of comfortable clean underwear at all times.

....

I randomly searched for "underwear rules for men" online and was pleasantly surprised about the results. The foremost feedback arrived at was about what type of underwear is suitable for men. Types like briefs, boxers, T-shirts and the like were mentioned. A hybrid "boxer briefs" was mostly touted as a more preferred type, as it gave a bit of both extremes of briefs and boxers.

An article in **MensHealth** by Hugh O'neill titled *The Rules: Loungewear, Win the over-and-under,* makes some interesting suggestions. He suggests, for example, that only 'cover models' should wear briefs, even though briefs project a more childish reminder. Hugh further suggests that a twice-a-year purge, (more like overhaul), is encouraged for a gentleman's wardrobe.

Light T-shirts as underwear are a good addition to a male wardrobe. Light colours such as white and light-grey are encouraged. However, black is also acceptable. It is more convenient to use 'V-neck' T-shirts where dress shirts are worn without a tie. However, a round neck is suitable.

Where T-shirts develop yellow armpit stains, it is suggested that usage of antiperspirants are discontinued and replaced with deodorants, says Hughs. He also suggests that non-chlorine bleach should be used to wash underwear for lasting effects.

Finally, are underwear compulsory? Is it wrong to avoid wearing underwear at all? Experts advise that underwear should be loose enough to allow enough air circulation around the scrotum, as ample circulation boosts and aids sperm production. Hence, not wearing underwear at all may have some good benefits.

However, an important aspect of using underwear is to package and appropriately keep the male organ in place to avoid unnecessary bulging and inappropriate disturbance. It is for a comfortable positioning of the male organ to present an accepted and tempered bulge of the frontage of pants/trouser or shorts.

RULE #15

General Clothing

Clothes, first and foremost, are to cover a man's nudity. The rest is to project an image, poise, personality and aura.
~ Senyo M. Adjabeng

....

There is a general convention for choice of clothing which is often driven by cultural and preferential factors. There is a psychological phenomenon called "clothed cognition" which involves the reflection of choice of clothing on a person's mood, health and overall confidence. Clothes basically cover a person's torso and feet and sometimes, head.

The choice of what we specifically choose to wear is somewhat preferential. In her February 2017 **HuffPost** article titled *How Clothing Choices Affect and Reflect your Self-Image,* Jill L. Ferguson states that "clothes can affect your success."

Knowing what effect clothes have on a person, how then and what should be the basic rules for choice of clothes for a perfect gentleman? Choice of colour of clothing comes into sharp focus. The choice of clothing colours stems from a person's skin tone or colour.

Skin tone may be 'Cool', 'Warm' or 'Neutral'. Cool skin tones rhyme with greens, blues and purple colour combinations, while Warm skin tones rhyme with reds, oranges, yellows, and yellow-green colour combinations. Neutral skin tones rhyme with dark and light greys, light and dark browns, navy and black colour combinations.

In clothing, colour is everything, and a perfect gentleman should endeavour to identify the colours that complement their body tone as well as project a confident and trendy personality. This is whether it is within the context of professional, casual, smart casual or ceremonial clothing as the case may be.

In all circumstances, a gentleman must dress appropriately to fit the occasion whether for ceremonial, business or informal engagements.

RULE #16

Suits

Well-fitting suits are Mandatory and a necessity for a gentleman's wardrobe. Suit accessories like ties, pocket squares, lapel pins, and 'chain-clocks' compliment personal style and charm, and a gentleman is encouraged to use them generously.

....

"Dressing well is a sign of good manners", says Tom Ford. This saying takes grooming to a whole new level for men especially. Dressing well is everything, and suits have become acceptable formal clothing across the world, with each continent designing their own unique styles.

About colour of suites, dark colours, (black, dark grey, blue black, coffee or other darker shades of blue), are convenient for business environments. Lighter shades are preferred for ceremonial and other formal occasions. Favorite business suits for many men are the dark shades of blue. Black suits are conservative and reserved for more formal business occasions, evening wear as well as funerals, and advisedly should be used sparingly.

On types of suits, a general classification will be Recreational, Ceremonial and Business Suits. Suit styles are mostly defined by the lapel, buttons and pockets. Generally, types of suits are also defined by number of pieces where a normal jacket and pants/trousers will be referred to as a two-piece suite, while a petty coat worn on a shirt and tie with a jacket and pants/trousers is referred to as a three-piece suit. Suits may also be single or double breasted

What constitutes a good suit? A suit is as good as how well it looks on a gentleman. A good looking suit is one which fits well. What then is a well-fitting suit?

1. Suit shoulders must sit on the wearer's shoulders firmly and smoothly.

2. Lapels must taper down from back of neck to the front of the torso. A suit that does not fit well will have a gap between the lapel and the shirt collar.

3. When a suit is closed, it must not fold at the sides. A well-fitting suit must allow for a full 'self-hug' without struggle.

4. Length of arm must align exactly with the wrist, and not drape unto or towards fingers, allowing for the tip of the shirt to peek-out.

5. Trouser/pants length must sit perfectly on shoes when standing with little or no folds, while suit jacket length must cover trouser/pants zipper or the buttocks.

However, a well-fitting suit without the right colour combination of shirt, tie and other complimentary accessories, may mar the looks of a good suit. As a general rule, darker suit colours must be combined with lighter coloured shirts. Ties must match and compliment the shirt colour and not necessarily the suit colour.

Suits are conservative clothing and leave very little room for adventure. The only freedom a gentleman gets while using complimentary accessories with a suit is the pocket square. Any colour of pocket square may be worn with any suit, and this is the only time a gentleman gets to be as adventurous as possible with assessor's colours around a suit.

Now, some general lifestyle rules regarding the wearing of suits. Thin lapels are trendier, and so are double vents at the back of a suit. Width of the tie must match the width of the lapel, and length of the tie must be in line with the belt or waist band of the trousers/pants.

Belts must be thin with a simple conventional buckle. For a trendy look, use a single button suit while trying on a double button for more formal wear. Suit must be unbuttoned before sitting down and must be buttoned on all or most other times.

Vests add a more formal look and are best worn with single breasted suits. Finally, the last button of a vest should always remain unbuttoned.

RULE #17

Footwear

Generally referred to as shoes, with variants such as boots, heels, sneakers, loafers, sandals and many other names.
A perfect gentleman carefully chooses shoes for two reasons –
1. For the perfect comfortable protection of the feet against "ground textures and temperature" and
2. for fashion and 'swagger'
~ trendy look.

....

"Footwear refers to garments worn on the feet…" (Wikipedia). This is a peculiar description of footwear which struck me in an exciting manner. I have never thought of shoes as 'garment'.

Different types of shoes are used for various occasions, and may be classified as for recreational, formal and business purposes.

While sneakers are often for sports related events, or smart casual wear for semi-formal occasions that allow for a sporty look, loafers are trendy shoes that can replace any casual shoe in a gentleman's shoe collection.

Though it is custom to wear loafers with socks, a trendier look recommends the wearing of loafers without socks, especially when worn with 'shorts'. Loafers are often worn with Jeans and Khakis. Loafers are lace-less and are not recommended for very formal wear whether for entertainment or business.

Various types of business shoes can be identified. One of the most popular is the Oxford shoe. There are also the Derby and Monk shoes. The difference between an Oxford shoe and a Derby shoe is that while Oxford shoes have closed lace straps, Derby shoes have open lace straps. Monk shoes, on the other hand, normally have buckle straps, and may be single or double strapped. The choice of shoe colour may be a matter of preference, and must specifically match with the colour of belt worn. As a grooming rule, shoe and belt colours must always match mandatorily.

Beyond colour, another factor that should affect the choice of shoes is the level of comfort. For this, a gentleman may want to consider choosing a shoe that is a size or half a size larger than a perfect fit. This allows for air and blood circulation around and within the feet.

Again, the specific sole chosen will often affect how comfortable a shoe may be. While a hard sole shoe may be a bit more rigid and unyielding at the sole, a soft sole may be more comfortable and flexible at the sole.

Derby Shoe

Oxford Shoe

Doble Strap Monk Shoe

Formal Loafer

RULE #18

Fragrance

"Good manners and good cologne is what transforms the man into a gentleman!"
~ Tom Ford

....

There is more to a perfect gentleman, and smelling good is one obvious characteristic. It does not only make a man more attractive, it is attraction in itself. Maurice Roucel said; "your fragrance is your message, your scented slogan."

Fragrance, in whatever shape or form, is a good and critical addition to a man's wardrobe. But, a common question I have often had to answer is what type of fragrance to wear, especially in the midst of a handful of unique types of fragrances for men, as well as the thousands of unique products and scents. I believe fragrances bond with specific personality types. In essence, they define a man's personality, be it mild, strong, or extremely strong.

Male fragrances come in Mists, Colognes, Perfumes and other uniquely 'cloned' fragrances. How do these differ from each other? Which is more powerful and lasts longer? And which is to be used and at what time? The difference in fragrances, as outlined above, stem from the amount or the concentration of perfume oils in the fragrance. The rest is often made of the base which may be water, alcohol and other additives. Mists contain the least amount of perfume oils of 2-3%, and hence evaporate very quickly after use in between 1-2 hours. Then there are the Colognes which carry between 5-9% of perfume oils and may last up to 6 hours, while pure perfumes and the strongest of fragrances may have up to 20% or more of perfume oil content.

So what makes fragrance? The answer is in the difference between fragrance oils and essential oils. While fragrance oils are inorganic and artificial, essential oils are organic and natural. Essential oils are often natural fragrant extracts from plants, roots, tree barks, leaves and sometimes flowers. The more difficult the extraction and processing of an essential oil, the more expensive it is.

Lavender is a special fragrance from the lavender tree or flowers which come from the mint family of plants. Hence, Lavender is a type of essential perfume oil and can also be artificially manufactured inorganically from a combination of compounds.

Hence, to grade the strength of fragrance in terms of the amount of perfume oil content, from low to high intensity and lasting power, we have the Body Mists (deodorant sprays/body splashes), then the Eau de Toilettes (milder version of Colognes), Eau de Cologne (Pure Colognes), Eau de Parfum and finally the strongest of them all, Perfume Oil, which can contain more than 20% of aromatic/perfume oils, whether essential or fragrant.

Where and how to wear perfumes

 Basically, the rule of wearing perfume is simple. Never spray perfumes directly into clothing; wear perfumes targeting all nooks and folds on the body such as the inner wrists, fore arms, on the chest and in-between the breasts, under the cheek bone, behind the ears etc. Target 1-3 areas at a time, but not all the areas at once.

Are there any downsides to wearing perfumes? Certainly. It is a matter of hygiene. Dermatology experts say fragrances on the body always leave 'toxic' residue on it when evaporation is complete. These have to be thoroughly washed off the body to avoid bad skin conditions, infections and even skin cancer in some extreme cases.

RULE #19

Mouth Care and Hygiene - the plaque

"Good manners and bad breath will get you nowhere."
~ Elvis Costello

O ne of the most terrible impressions you can leave with anyone is bad breath. Every time they think about their moment with you, the only thing that will linger on their mind is the discomfort and nausea they felt after inhaling a stinking smell from your mouth. As a gentleman, it is important to develop a good mouth care routine.

Brushing your teeth twice a day could be a great way to help you ensure good breath. The use of mouth wash also helps ensure fresh breath. After eating a dish that could cause an uncomfortable breath, it is advisable to chew a gum as this could help reduce the smell the dish may have left behind.

When brushing your teeth, ensure you pay attention to your tongue area as well. It will not hurt to visit the dentist at least twice in a year, to ensure everything is all good with your teeth.

Some gentlemen ignore their lips most of the time, with the assumption that it's a feminine thing to want to have smooth shiny lips. Dear gentleman, forget about 'shiny' but you can always use a little Vaseline or shea butter on your lips to prevent them from cracking as a result of dryness.

RULE #20

Accessories: Shirt Stays, Belts, and other Accessories

"Accessories are like vitamins to fashion - as such, you should use them liberally".
~ Anna Dello Russo

....

A rule of thumb for a perfect gentleman: " Clothes make people."

Clothing accessories are items used to complete an outfit and complement clothing. They have the capacity to further express an individual's identity and personality.

Shirt stays are elastic straps that connect the bottom of a dress-shirt to the socks or feet. Their objective is to hold the shirt in place and tacked in, without coming out of the trousers. The purpose is to keep the dress-shirt tucked in all the time.

There are two main varieties; those that loop around the foot and those that clip onto the sock. All varieties have two clips at the top; one for the front and one for the back of the shirt.

The choice of a neck tie is not only an art but a science; ties must be carefully chosen to rhyme with the shirt on which it is worn. A perfect gentleman must learn how to knot a tie and store neck ties away knotted and ready for use.

The following are some basic rules of wearing a tie

The neck-tie and the shirt should be complimentary in colour and not seem busy.

Neck ties cannot have the same pattern as the shirt.

The tip of the tie should barely touch your belt buckle and never go below it.

Ex-American President, Donald Trump, is well-known for ties, and has been cited on occasion to be in constant breach of this rule.

Leather belts hold up pants or trousers to give an enhanced polished look, with sleek tans and shiny buckles. It is essential for a gentleman to pick the right type of belt to match an outfit. Basic rule of thumb is the colour of leather belt should match the leather shoe. Buckles should be simple and conservative but classic.

Belts for 'Cowboy' outfits such as jeans may have bigger buckles.

A perfect gentleman should make the effort to use all other clothing accessories in moderation, unless such outfit is culturally motivated by type, by theme and by occasion. Rings, Hats and scarfs are all complimentary items to the specific clothing type and style.

Finally, does a gentleman choose tattoos and piercings as complimentary accessories or not? I believe the simple answer should be limited to culture and preference. A perfect gentleman should choose wisely with the view to looking good, confident, appealing and influential.

PART 3:
RELATIONSHIPS

"Human relationships are primary in all of living. When the gusty winds blow and shake our lives, if we know that people care about us, we may bend with the wind…. but we won't break."
~ Fred Rogers

RULE #21

Friends

"Life is partly what we make it, and partly what it is made by the friends we choose."
~ Tennessee Williams

....

Jess C. Scott says, "Friends are the family you choose."

Unlike family, we get to choose our friends. It's often said, "show me your friend and I will show you your character," and that, "birds of the same feather flock together." Clearly, friends define us Friends brand us. A perfect gentleman has a choice, opportunity and liberty in choosing friends who complete him.

A perfect gentleman should have three (3) categories of friends at a time; a set of younger friends who look up to him and he mentors and coaches, a set of friends as colleagues he shares his life and challenges with, and a set of older friends who guide, advise and share their rich experiences with him. A perfect gentleman must have at least one older friend who he looks up to and draws inspiration from.

In his words, Henry Ford describes and captures the nature of a best friend when he says, "My best friend is the one who brings out the best in me." "My best friend is the man who in wishing me well, wishes it for my sake," Aristotle adds.

"The most beautiful discovery true friends make is that they can grow separately without growing apart."

~ Elisabeth Foley

RULE #22

The First Date

"A person's readiness to date is largely a matter of maturity and environment."
~ Myles Munroe

....

The first date is everything. The success of the first date usually determines whether there is a second which could lead to a beautiful relationship. In our contemporary world, mobile phones and social media enables potential couples to communicate at length before a first date. I guess things are much easier and better than during the time of our fathers.

But what should a gentleman look out for on a first date? A date may be many things but certainly not an interview. Getting to spend time and to know each other a bit more shouldn't be such a big deal. It should be a casual and interactive private time together.

A perfect gentleman shows up on time, clean, smelling 'good' and has a comfortable and confident outlook on a first date. A fresh breath is indeed a must. Venue is normally tricky. Both may easily agree on a conducive place, or where the gentleman is choosing, the place must compliment the lady's personality. A unique place that engenders good memories, new experiences, connectedness and above all emotional exchanges should be perfect for a first date. The venue must create unique opportunities for communicating and talking enough with little or no interference.

The **Pick-up:** A gentleman picks up his lady for a first date. Often, if driving, he parks his car in the lady's driveway, walks to the front door, rings the bell and goes in to escort his date back to the car. A gentleman is required to open the car door for his date, shutting the door gently after the lady is comfortably seated in the front seat and walks around the car to resume his seat. Where there is a driver, the driver may hold the door open for both with the lady entering the vehicle (back seat) first.

Mannerism: A first date is a platform for a showcase of what a gentleman is and stands for - personality, poise, professionalism and humorous companionship. A gentleman must show confidence, a sense of control and a general awareness of social norms and values. On a first date, a perfect gentleman speaks in a tempered tone, in confidence and with a gentle soothing voice that depicts care, romance and admirable masculinity.

The Menu: Choosing the most appropriate meal from the menu can be tricky at times. Generally, both are required to choose their own meal from the menu but often, the lady may choose to defer to the choice of the gentleman. It is important to have an idea about her preferred taste so that a gentleman may be in a position to make suggestions if required to. Simple meals are recommended. Complex meals such as pasta or crabs which takes some expertise to eat without being messy, are to be avoided. Again, the first date is not a place for experimenting new dishes unless it is so agreed. Meanwhile, make room for dessert since a lady on a first date will surely appreciate a good desert.

The Conversation: What is a safe conversation on a first date? Generally the aim of a first date is to know each other a bit more. So subject matter that focuses on personal attributes, likes, dislikes, preferences, etc. are encouraged. But care must be taken not to probe to the extent where the other feels their privacy is overly encroached, obtrusive or infringed upon.

The Cheque: Who gets the Bill during a date? Generally the gentleman picks up the bill on a first date and just be prepared for same. This is often because he invited the lady. In our contemporary world however, some ladies may insist on sharing the bill or taking the full bill, especially if they invited the gentleman. A gentleman should insist on taking the full bill, but must be ready to yield where there is a strong insistent from the lady. A simple matter as who picks up the bill should not ruin a perfect date.

Drop Off: A perfect gentleman drops of his date especially on a first date. At worst, the gentleman must make transport arrangements to ensure that the lady gets home safe. The ideal however will be for the gentleman to drop off the lady and walk her to her front door and make sure she is safely inside before leaving. It is a matter of responsibility and security also.

The Kiss and Intimacy: Often at the tail end of a good first date, the question arises whether to kiss or not. The kiss on a first date is a big deal where some men insist on it and some women expect it. A first date need not end up in a kiss as a 'sine qua non'. If it is mutually yearned then it is a matter of consent between two adults. A first date that does not end up in a kiss does not make a bad or failed first date as some gentlemen may believe.

I was on a date with this really hot model. Well, it wasn't really a date. We just ate dinner and saw a movie. Then the plane landed.
~ Dave Attell

RULE #23

Etiquette at the Table

Eating is aggressive by nature, and the implements required for it could quickly become weapons; table manners are, most basically, a system of taboos designed to ensure that violence remains out of the question.
~ Margaret Visser

. . . .

Table manners and etiquette are one of the foremost things a perfect gentleman must master; it is not negotiable. We eat all the time. Sometimes, three times or more every day. Eating in style and with finesse is a characteristic of a fine-cultured gentleman.

The first is the handling of the table napkin, which is certainly not for cleaning sweat off the face but for table sanitary purposes, for the cleaning of the hands and mouth. The next is the cutlery. A perfect gentleman must learn to pick and use the right cutlery for the right meals and deserts at table.

Another important etiquette is mannerism at table. A gentleman's rule is to ensure that you address everyone politely at table, avoid stuffing the mouth, chew slowly, cover the mouth when you cough at table and limit the excessive movement of hands when you communicate. By all means, a gentleman avoids placing elbows on the table as much as possible.

Another gentleman's rule at table is to be polite and helpful to everyone, lowering the voice and not talk with food in your mouth and generally avoid being messy. Spitting and loud chewing noises should certainly be avoided.

The table is not a place for arguments. However, it can represent a forum for effective communication and resolution of differences. Food indeed brings people together.

The dinner table is the center for the teaching and practicing not just of table manners but of conversation, consideration, tolerance, family feeling, and just about all the other accomplishments of polite society except the minuet.
~ Judith Martin

RULE #24

Cooking

I love life. I love to cook.
~ Senyo M. Adjabeng

. . . .

It has always been admirable watching a man cook... especially an accomplished gentleman. There has always been the misconception that cooking is the duty of a woman. There is nothing more romantic than a gentleman who knows his wine and can cook.

A perfect gentleman should be able to cook, at least as a matter of his own security and survival skills. Cooking is therapeutic and liberating. At best, it provides a major attainment of independence from the manipulation of a woman.

Everyone can learn how to cook. Julia Shild said, "...no one is born a great cook, one learns by doing."

"Cooking is at once child's play and adult joy. And cooking done with care is an act of love."
~ Craig Claiborne

RULE #25

Wine and Liquor

"It provokes the desire, but it takes away the performance"
~ William Shakespeare

....

It was Napoleon Bonaparte that once said, "Nothing makes the future look so rosy as to contemplate it through a glass of Chambertin."

It is said that a glass of wine a day keeps the crazy at bay. Similarly, another rendition states that a glass of wine a day is good for you. Of course, health experts have enumerated several benefits of wine, especially red wine. But is alcohol really good for man? Is alcohol man's friend as is commonly said?

This is one of the grey areas of life where everyone argues from their own corner of right and wrong, and both can be right or wrong, depending on the circumstances.

Alcohol is as complicated a subject matter as love is. Alcohol is a typical subject matter where those who consume it admire those who don't, and those who don't sometimes wish they did, and thus admire those who do. The decision to take alcohol or not is a tricky choice for a perfect gentleman.

The worse description a gentleman should avoid is to be referred to as one who has 'a drinking problem'. To be a man is to be in control of one's life. What excessive alcohol does is to steal away control of life ever so subtly.

By all means, enjoy life and live it to the fullest and finest. If that includes consumption of wine and or liquor, fine. But, never lose control. A rule of thumb for the perfect gentleman is moderation, if you ever choose to consume alcohol.

Obviously, alcohol is a big deal for most. Chelsea Handler said, "There are two kinds of people I don't trust: people who don't drink and people who collect stickers." "Alcohol may be man's worst enemy, but the Bible says love your enemy," says Frank Sinatra.

The ability to avoid the consumption of alcohol is a virtue. Yet, the consumption of same may not be vice. As Matt Greoning puts it, "To alcohol! The cause of... and solution to... all of life's problems"

Excessive alcohol kills. Excessive alcohol destroys. There is no two ways about that. A perfect gentleman must surely be aware of this and choose wisely.

"I love everything that is old; old friends, old times, old manners, old books, old wines."
~ Oliver Goldsmith

RULE #26

Smoking

My rule of life prescribed as an absolutely sacred rite smoking cigars and also the drinking of alcohol before, after and if need be, during all meals and in the intervals between them.
~ Winston Churchill

....

Smoking is bad for your health. That is the most common phrase you'll get in recent times. Our fathers enjoyed their good tobacco until the tobacco industry underwent major social backlash and pushed back. It was trendy then to smoke. Today, many laws and regulations have been passed against smoking especially, in most public places.

Smoking is agreeably a bad habit and is addictive. Most people I have met who smoke largely wish they could quit. Some young men pick up the smoking habit as early as their pre-teen ages and often smoke, unable to quit for the rest of their lives.

A perfect gentleman should avoid smoking where possible, where it is already a habit, a desperate attempt to completely stop smoking or at worst to drastically reduce the frequency of smoking.

The rule for a perfect gentleman who chooses to smoke should be moderation. Everything in moderation is good health advise. Sugar, Milk, Coffee, Carbohydrates, Meat or alcohol, all may be harmful, if not consumed in moderation.

Always ensure, should you find yourself smoking, that you smoke in areas that are designated as smoking areas.

"A woman is only a woman, but a good cigar is a smoke"
~ Rudyard Kipling.

RULE #27

The First Kiss

I am a strong believer in kissing being very intimate, and the minute you kiss, the floodgates open for everything.
~ Jennifer Lopez.

....

A first kiss is a nightmare, just ask every young man. I remember my first kiss like it was yesterday. A good first kiss is a confidence booster, and a bad first kiss can be devastating to a personality for life. Taken for granted, a first kiss can never be made right or compensated for.

Yet, a first kiss in the life of a young man (no man gets their first kiss in old age) can be frightening, fearful and tense. A perfect first kiss is often one that is rehearsed. Be it a few simple moments before the mirror every now and then, mimicking lip and mouth movements, practicing with a doll, or asking tips from female friends, a perfect gentleman must prepare for the first kiss.

The perfect first kiss does magic to a gentleman's ego, that ultimate feeling of a man.

What should you expect in a first kiss? Hermann Hesse responds. "At the first kiss, I felt something melt inside me that hurt in an exquisite way. All my longings, all my dreams and sweet anguish, all the secrets that slept deep within me came awake, everything was transformed and enchanted, everything made sense."

Is it ever worth it? Yes! Especially if the first lady is 'the special lady'. A first kiss should never be wasted away in flippant haste. The conclusion of the matter is for a perfect gentleman to ensure that the first kiss is for the woman he truly loves.

"I think Heaven will be like a first kiss."
~ Sarah Addison Allen

RULE #28

Lovers Living-in and Cohabitation

Consequently, cohabitation becomes an acceptable halfway relationship, which can be dissolved more easily than a marriage.
~Wang Xun

……………………………………………………..

A live-in arrangement is where an unmarried couple live together in a long-term relationship under one roof. It is also often referred to as cohabitation.

Cohabitation has become more common in many parts of the world as a result of rapid urbanisation and other social factors. Where two people of the opposite sex meet each other and fall in love, they want to be together and see each other all the time or as much as possible. This may lead to the haste to move in with each other.

In some jurisdictions, cohabitation for a period can constitute a legal spousal relationship. A perfect gentleman must become aware and not blinded by the immediate feelings to make the hasty decision of cohabitation.

Living-in with a lover may have the best of intentions and some immediate positive outlook. However, as relationships drag and love gets tested over time, the decision may begin to look washed and hastily applied. Some lovers cohabitate successfully and end up married. But, the reality is that not all such arrangements work out. Indeed, many fail.

A perfect gentleman is one who chooses wisely. Charbel Tadros said, "Some people are not meant to live together, for they will destroy one another and annihilate themselves. Wolves and sheep cannot be put in the same place, for after eating the sheep, the wolves will starve to death."

Marcel Proust adds, "When you come to live with a woman, you will soon cease to see anything of what made you love; though it is true that the two sundered elements can be reunited by jealousy."

"I'll share my life with you. But, not my doughnuts."
~ Crystal Woods

RULE # 29

Lovers as Business Partners

"A friendship founded on business is better than a business founded on friendship."
~ John D. Rockefeller

....

It is difficult to be objective when it comes to affairs of the heart. In this era of entrepreneurship, it is not a bad idea for couples to want to start a business venture together. However, it is important for the lovers to know that a decision such as this could be both ugly and good and should be ready to deal with it.

Truth is that not all couples or all relationships thrive from working together. So, a perfect gentleman ensures that leisure is separated from work as efficiently as possible.

As friends, learn to share business goals and support each other. Make it a point to appreciate each other for a job well done, and be kind about how you approach constructive criticism.

Is it beneficial to choose to go into a business partnership with your partner? It makes more sense if the relationship is legalized as in Marriage. Where there is no legal basis for the relationship, it may be difficult to recoup your investments in the business. Hence, if he so chooses to go that way, a perfect gentleman should properly arrange for a professionally contracted, well-articulated and understood business relationship, aside the social friendship or sexual relationship.

Some couples have made awesome business partners. A perfect gentleman, on a case by case circumstantial basis, must think carefully and choose wisely.

"Friends don't always make the best of business partners."
~ Chris Campbell

RULE #30

Resolving Relationship Disputes

"Peace is not the absence of conflict; it is the ability to handle conflict by peaceful means."
~ Ronald Reagan

....

Any man very soon realises that disagreements and disputes cannot be kept at bay. Disagreements and disputes are inevitable. Indeed, it is ok to be upset, but self-control is the true mark of a perfect gentleman.

Like a diplomat, handle all disagreements with tact, poise and deliberate execution. Maintain a calm and respectful demeanour during heated conversations.

Try to find an objective middle ground in the midst of a dispute. Holding unto one's position only promotes and worsens the dispute. Rather, compromising or the willingness to compromise is key to resolving disputes. Endeavour to listen to the other party. Listening is not the same as hearing; when we listen, we dedicate full mental attention to what is being communicated. Good listening skills is epitomised in a mature, emotionally intelligent man.   Listening allows for effective communication.

A lack of communication, miscommunication or the absence of communication is the cause of many disputes. A perfect gentleman is the one who is willing and ready to apologize when in the wrong. Eating the humble pie is gentlemanly when it becomes clear that one is in the wrong. An apology is a powerful antidote to prolonged dispute.

By all means, a gentleman should stand his ground and make his point, but where wrong, he must be ready to apologize and retract anything wrongly said, or any actions of omission or commission.

"Arguing with somebody is never pleasant, but sometimes it is useful and necessary to do so."
~Lemony Snicket

PART 4
SPIRITUALITY

Spirituality: the art of keeping your internal fire alive.
~ Maxime Lagacé

RULE #31

The Good Book

DO NOT LET THIS BOOK OF THE LAW DEPART FROM YOUR MOUTH. YOU SHALL MEDITATE UPON IT DAY AND NIGHT AND BE CAREFUL TO DO ALL THAT IS WRITTEN IN IT. AND YOU SHALL BECOME SUCCESSFUL.

~ Joshua 1: 8 (The Holy Bible - NIV)

There are laws that govern our day to day lives as human beings. More so, as Christians, the Bible has been made available to help us live a life worthy and acceptable in the sight of God.

As Christians, we believe our ultimate source is God, and He, in His infinite wisdom, has made everything available to us through Christ Jesus, if only we will believe and have faith. Now, the Good Book says that faith cometh by hearing and hearing of the word of God. This is why it is important to make it a point as a gentleman to meditate on the word of God.

You can't give what you don't have. Therefore, as a human being, to be able to exude a certain character or trait, you have to constantly practice. By studying the Word, we are empowered to do the impossible.

RULE #32

The God Factor

"And the Peace of God that surpasses all understanding, will guard your hearts and minds through Christ Jesus.

~ Philippians 4: 7 (The Holy Bible)
…………………………………………………………………..

Religion is believed to be an organized system of beliefs and practice. However, spirituality is not linked to any religious institution or organization. Spirituality is "the feelings, thoughts, experiences and behaviours that arise from a search of the sacred".

The ability to come to the conscious belief that there is a supreme being (God), in itself is gentlemanly. Atheists do not believe in the supernatural or the existence of God. The belief in 'nothingness' is at best hollow, especially when science struggles and fails to explain everything.

A perfect gentleman should make meaning of life and its aftermath within the context of a supernatural superior being, God, who controls the unexplainable.
Choose to be religious or not. However, certainly be

spiritual. The non-physical needs more than a mortal mind to transcend.

RULE #33

Prayer

Don't pray when you feel like it. Have an appointment with the Lord and keep it. A man is powerful on his knees
~ Corrie Ten Boom

....

Prayer is a consistent communication with 'God'. Bishop T. D. Jakes also said, "She (my mother) became a warrior far superior to any epic hero. She became a giant on her knees. With a sword in one hand, she battled the enemies of death and disease, and with her other hand stretched toward heaven she kept beseeching God's help and His mercy."

Billy Graham said, "True prayer is a way of life, not just for use in cases of emergency. Make it a habit, and when the need arises, you will be in practice."

So prayer must be a lifestyle, not just a backup plan. There is a God, a supreme being that controls nature and brings meaning to life and its aftermath.
A perfect gentleman is one who seeks the godly path, a

path to righteousness and divinity.

"To be a Christian without prayer is no more possible than to be alive without breathing."
~ Martin Luther

RULE # 34

Charity

"The smallest act of kindness is worth more that the grandest intention."
~ Oscar Wilde

....

The act of giving freely is not a science, and neither is it an art. It is a conviction and an attitude. Charity rises above self in the interest of another, mostly more vulnerable than one's self.

A perfect gentleman is one who gives freely back to the society that made him. It is consciousness based on the conviction that some people may need what we do not need. It is based on the conviction that others deserve a little of what we can afford to lose - to do without.

So, a perfect gentleman should give from the abundance of the heart and the graciousness of his goodness. Charity begins from the conscientiousness of the heart - HOME.
A perfect gentleman is a true giver.

"It's not how much we give but how much love we put into giving."
~ Mother Theresa

RULE #35

Morality

"When the whole world is running towards a cliff, he who is running in the opposite direction appears to have lost his mind."
~C. S Lewis

....

Morality is the principle of distinguishing between right and wrong.

The forces of life hardly teach the difference between right and wrong or good and evil. Somehow, from birth, we tend to know the difference subconsciously. Immorality, in contemporary usage and understanding, has been limited to actions or inactions, commissions or omissions of sexual impropriety.

Immorality, the act of being morally complicit, goes way beyond sexual action. It is simply the evil that men do. Doing right or wrong is a choice men make as life throws its icy challenges at them.

A perfect gentleman is one who chooses the path of

morality; doing right to all manner of people without distinction. Moral uprightness is gentlemanly.

However, the line between morality and immorality has become too thin in recent times. What may be immoral and unacceptable in one culture and community may be moral and acceptable in another.

It confuses many a well-meaning gentleman as to which way to tread, for sometimes evil and bad immoral conduct seems to pay more. Henry David Thoreau said, "Do not be too moral. You may cheat yourself out of much life. So aim above morality. Be not simply good, be good for something."

For a perfect gentleman, a principal moral code should be to always do unto others what he wishes on himself.

"I am free; no matter what rules surround me. If I find them tolerable, I tolerate them; if I find them too obnoxious, I break them. I am free because I know that I alone am morally responsible for everything I do."
~ Robert A. Heinlein

RULE #36

Love for Others

"Love is that condition in which the happiness of another person is essential to your own."
– Robert A. Heinlein

....

Some say that Love is the most powerful force that exists, that love is eternal.

The love between a mother and her baby, the love between 'lovers', the love a doctor has for a patient, the love shared among friends, the love between a teacher and students, all tell us that love is universal.

Agape Love (divine love for mankind), Erotic Love (of sexuality), Phileo Love (brotherly love, of friends and equals) and Storge Love (of family - parents and children), manifest in strong feelings of affection, trust and total openness, loyalty and vulnerability to the other.

Showing love is not a sign of weakness. Rather, it is of control, of balance and equilibrium within oneself.

However, the exhibition of love is a risk, as it may be subjected to rejection and 'heartbreak' by the other - an act of utmost betrayal of love.

A perfect gentleman must love at all cost, but ever so wisely. Many have been driven to their graves from the betrayal of love. Instead of loving many, love but a few.

C.S. Lewis said, "To love at all is to be vulnerable. Love anything and your heart will be wrung and possibly broken. If you want to make sure of keeping it intact you must give it to no one, not even an animal. Wrap it carefully round with hobbies and little luxuries; avoid all entanglements. Lock it up safe in the casket or coffin of your selfishness. But in that casket, safe, dark, motionless, airless, it will change. It will not be broken; it will become unbreakable, impenetrable, irredeemable. To love is to be vulnerable."

I choose to love. Very well aware of the risk, I still choose to love again and again, knowing I may get hurt again and again. I will love the 11th time after 10 heartbreaks, knowing I may be hurt again, and surely continue to love.

"In the end nothing we do or say in this lifetime will matter as much as the way we have loved one another".
~Daphne Rose Kingma

RULE #37

Duty of Care

"Compassion is the basis of morality"
~Arthur Schopenhauer

....

A perfect gentleman must understand the true meaning of duty of care; it basically refers to an obligation imposed on an individual, which requires adherence to reasonable care.

Duty of care may also be considered a formalization of the duties an individual has towards others in the society. Care is described as expressing worry, paying close attention, showing concern or responsibility towards an object or a living being. The acts of Care can be seen in love for animals as pets, people in a relationship or marriage, before, during and after delivery of babies, attending to a depressed, sick or aged person.

To place the needs, worries and sentiments of others before yours as a perfect gentleman, does not make you weak or reduce your value as a person, but rather increases the respect people have for you.

If your actions are likely to adversely affect someone else, then you owe them a duty of care. This essentially means you have to take reasonable care to ensure that those people are not harmed or injured, as a result of the things you choose to do.

The moment a gentleman ignores his duty of care, it can be said to be an act of negligence. Duty of care is a duty of conscientiousness.

"You can't, in sound morals, condemn a man for taking care of his own integrity. It is his clear duty."
~ Joseph Conrad

RULE #38

Polygamy

"Polygamy: An endeavour to get more out of life than there is in it"
~Elbert Hubbard

....

Unlike Christianity, some religions such as Islam endorse Polygamy.

Whether a man believes in or succumbs to the principles of Polygamy or not, the critical objective should be to assume responsibility for mother and child to secure and protect the future of humanity. Not to limit this to any religion, teaching, prophecy, or theory, any man who decides he wants to have more than a wife should be a gentleman enough to be a husband to each of them.

The debate about the morality of keeping several wives (polygamy) as against one wife (monogamy) has raged for several decades and perhaps centuries. However, I see it in quite a simple context. A man chooses whether to keep a large family or a small one. This, he may do through the influence of culture, religion or family history.

A large family may be achieved through a single wife and many children or several wives with children. It is a unique decision every man makes and should make at some point in life.

In deciding to keep a large family, a man must ensure that none of the wives feels cheated, and each one is equally respected and loved, though that is always a tall order.

A man married to more than one woman is likely to deal with a bit of disturbance of peace from time to time; it is his responsibility to ensure there is peace and harmony in his home. In the process of resolving issues, he should try as much as possible to remain neutral and objective.

A perfect gentleman takes care of family; family comes first. The choice to whether pursue and keep a big or small family, or one or several wives, is a personal decision a man must make. However, the critical condition is to be able to fend for all of them.

Another consideration may be that of control. A man who chooses to keep a large family must endeavour to keep control to prevent disputes, for disputes will abound in keeping a large family, whether with one wife and several children or with several wives.

To avoid all the above complications of life, some writers, philosophers, scholars and even religious teachers advise against marrying more than one wife.

Tom Robbins said, "When we're incomplete, we're always searching for somebody to complete us. When, after a few years or a few months of a relationship, we find that we're still unfulfilled, we blame our partners and take up with somebody more promising.

This can go on and on – several cases of polygamy - until we admit that while a partner can add sweet dimension to our lives, each of us are responsible for our own fulfilment. Nobody else can provide it for us, and to believe otherwise is to delude ourselves dangerously and to program ourselves for eventual failure in every relationship we enter."

Each one for himself. Monogamy or polygamy, a large or small family, is always a choice that should be considered carefully. Both, however, do not insulate a perfect gentleman from the complications of life and family.

"Polygamy is a luxury of the cave-people, and monogamy is an existential responsibility of the civilized society."

~ Abhijit Naskar, Wise Mating: A Treatise on Monogamy

RULE #39

Inspiration

"Inspiration responds to our attentiveness in various and sometimes unexpected ways"
~Wayne W. Dyer

....

Everyone is inspired by something or someone. I am inspired by the personalities of my father, Nelson Mandela, and Barack Obama. Their lives, motivation, integrity, leadership careers and utterances inspire me.

I am further inspired by music, nature and the Bible. Others are inspired by other things and persons.
A perfect gentleman should draw inspiration from something or someone.

Inspiration is that deep feeling of awakening and energy that grips a person upon reading, listening, hearing or observing a person or thing they love or admire, which leads to a strong motivation to do anything....to want to live meaningfully and successfully.

When inspired, there is no limit to what a gentleman can achieve.

RULE #40

Death and the After-life

"Death is not the opposite of life, but a part of it"
~Haruki Murakami

....

Death is an inevitable aspect of our lives; everyone at a point in time has lost a dear one.

The thought of death is frightening. Yet it remains a fact that we are all bound to die. A perfect gentleman is one who recognises the fact and reality of death, embraces it, prepares for it and answers the question of the afterlife. The first most important thing to do is to make a will. A will is not essentially meant to distribute property but also to communicate what should happen upon one's death. Writing a will gives you the opportunity to determine what should happen when you are no more, and makes it easier for loved ones to cope after you are gone.

A typical example will be to indicate how your burial should be carried and other important things you wish to be done upon your passing. Consult a family lawyer to assist with a will at your earliest convenience.

Another important question to answer is how your loved ones will cope in your absence. A perfect gentleman provides financial and other security for loved ones when they pass. Every day of life should be lived with the knowledge of the possibility of death. A perfect gentleman prepares for such an eventuality by ensuring that some arrangements such as investments, trust, savings and other similar arrangements remain to cater for loved ones.

Finally, a perfect gentleman should try to answer the question 'what happens after death'? This question will often lead to the search for a spiritual identity. Christians believe there is judgement after death and the existence of a heaven for the 'saved' and the 'chosen', and hell for the 'sinner' and the 'rejected'.

The answer for the afterlife is a matter of belief and faith, and a perfect gentleman must explore and come to a firm resolution and absolute belief of his fate afterlife. When you choose, be sure it is a choice which brings you peace and that which gives you the confidence to accept and embrace death as the ultimate end of life.

"We all die. The goal isn't to live forever; the goal is to create something that will" ~Chuck Palahniuk

PART 5

PROFESSIONALISM

I have worked with some of the most important players, like Ronaldo, Ibrahimovic, Kaka, Zidane, but the best are easy to work with because they are so professional. Their winning mentality, professionalism, helps the manager. Of course, sometimes I become angry, but usually my relationship with the players is calm.

~ Carlo Ancelotti

RULE #41

Leadership and Influence

"Leadership is influence, nothing more and nothing less"
~John Maxwell

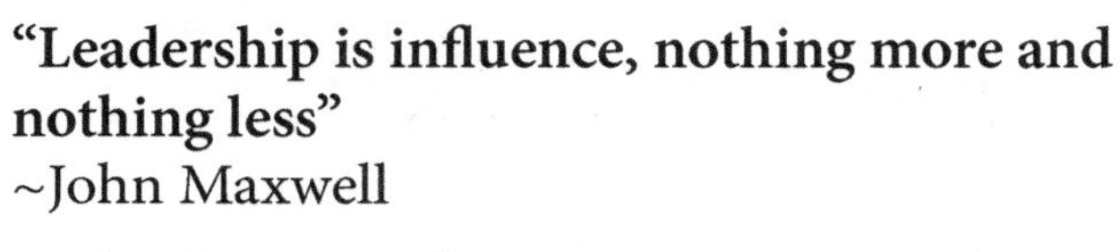

eadership evolves from an opportunity to influence others towards meeting a personal, organizational or communal goal. Leaders emerge from opportunistic situations accidentally or deliberately, meaning they can be, become and be made.

No matter how a leader emerges, a great leader is one that helps his or her followers to appreciate the goal towards which all are working while discovering themselves. A perfect gentleman is aware that a leadership position is a position of opportunity for achievement and positive impact, and not for selfish gain or benefit.

A leader without influence is less likely to get followers to act in the ways they ought to. Being a great leader of influence means followers have absolute confidence and loyalty in the leader and are willing to listen and act on the leader's behest.

A perfect gentleman seeks every opportunity to discover his natural talent and ability on the lifelong journey. Leadership is not a stagnant process, it is continuous and demands daily discovery of oneself.

"Leaders become great not because of their power but, because of their ability to empower others".
~John C. Maxwell

RULE #42

Presentation Skills

"Words have incredible power. They can make people's hearts soar or they can make people's hearts sore".
~Dr Mardy Grothe

....

Presentation skills... the power of communicating at great effect.

A gentleman communicates with precision and avoids doubts, confusion or chaos. It is prudent to consider who the audience is/are, the purpose of delivery and the feedback anticipated. Presentation is not just communicating, it is communicating for a specific purpose and objective. Good communication is to elicit specific feedback or promote a particular agenda successfully.

To handle a presentation effectively, it is ideal to use the 3 Es' in Public Speaking; **Energy** (vibe), **Enthusiasm** (activeness) and **Engagement** (creativity, flair).

Humour and the use of storytelling or illustrations has been the hallmark of many powerful presentations. Delivering a key message while entertaining an audience works very often.

A perfect gentleman's presentations are crafted to just 'Keep It Short and Simple' (KISS). When presentations are short and accurate, they leave the audience with memories that will make them yearning for more.

"Make sure you have finished speaking before your audience has finished listening."
~Dorothy Sarnoff.

RULE #43

Meetings

"A great person attracts great people and knows how to hold them together"
~ Johann Von Goethe

....

Meetings are places where great minds meet. Meetings reveal who we are, what we are made up of and what we have to contribute. Meetings are about sharing ideas and those who have a lot to say or share are those who are well prepared. Preparation for every meeting, big or small, relevant or irrelevant, urgent or ordinary is essential.

A perfect gentleman arrives at meetings on time. This is not negotiable as it shows professionalism, good conduct and commitment. The other essential is the choice of clothes. Good grooming and looks attracts respect, admiration and attention in a meeting as people are willing to listen.

A perfect gentleman arrives at meetings well prepared,

aware of the purpose of a meeting, whether it's an informing (straightforward formal discussions where information is given), consulting (discussions of policies and innovations for crosschecking and implementation of ideas), problem solving (description of problems and providing solutions to solve problems) or decision making (analysis of problems, drawing and implementation of ideas for solutions).

Meetings have a structured format. A gentleman must be aware of the format and align accordingly. Before tackling the agenda for the day's meeting, meetings will often begin with a review of previous minutes, then a discussion of matters arising and finally an adoption of the minutes as authentic record of proceedings of previous meeting. The agenda of the day's meeting can then be undertaking ending in any other relevant matters other than those outlined on the day's agenda.

Meetings usually provide an avenue for networking, negotiations, exchange of ideas and the discovery of new ideas. A perfect gentleman must endeavour to take away key lessons and outcomes from each and every meeting, especially activities responsible for and things to follow up and report in subsequent future meetings.

A perfect gentleman utilises meetings to achieve

personal career goals, deepen professional networks and improve personal and technical knowledge.

''Networking is an essential part of building wealth''.
~ Armstrong Williams

RULE #44

Managing Time

"Your time is limited, so don't waste it living someone else's life. Don't be trapped by dogma – which is living with the results of other people's thinking. Don't let the noise of other's opinions drown out your own inner voice. And most important, have the courage to follow your heart and intuition. They somehow already know what you truly want to become. Everything else is secondary."
~ Steve Jobs

. . . .

Time is a leveller, no respecter of persons and gives all equal opportunities for proper utilisation or wastage. Time allows for decision making, planning and control of self-worth without distinction. A perfect gentleman manages time effectively.

Prioritising **tasks** ensures maximum use of time, prevents tardiness and confusion. A perfect gentleman prioritises urgent and time dependent tasks while scheduling other important but non-urgent activities more randomly and casually.

Work never finishes, always beckoning and engaging at all times and a perfect gentleman apportions time effectively to have a perfect or at least a near perfect work-life balance. The essence of a good life is not that which is drowned in excessive work but rather a fine balance between work and leisure.

A perfect gentleman spends sometime with friends, colleagues, and acquaintances and especially family. Schedule fun-time and vacations with friends and family ensuring we have some good memories of life together with those we care about. Time must be spent to make essential memories for the future so that when we are frail and immobile in old age, we can at least garner fond memories of the past and still enjoy the times.

Life is short and a perfect gentleman remembers to celebrate even the smallest successes. It is just as important as work to set aside time to celebrate the smallest things that happen in our lives.

We are the masters of our own time and same makes us a good life or otherwise.

"The bad news is time flies, but the good news is you are the pilot".
~Micheal Althsuler

RULE #45
Managing the Boss

I am thankful for all those difficult people in my life. They have shown me exactly who I do not want to be. ~ Al. E Gater

. . . .

Everyone has a boss. So does the perfect gentleman. Bosses come in all shapes and forms. Some are nice and some are mean. Some are helpful and others destructive. Some are supportive and others downright hostile, antagonistic and becoming the source of frustration, abuse and disrespect.

The general rule of being a good follower is to say nothing when there's nothing good to say about the leader or boss. A perfect gentleman exercises great wisdom in showing an open and optimistic attitude towards the boss whether the boss acknowledges efforts or not.

It is important to know the boss's communication style and adjust accordingly. This makes interactions much easier and smoother with little or no friction. A perfect gentleman therefore knows when and how to discuss problems with the boss.

It is advisable to take a moment to have an intended conversation with the boss in your head, gauge the appropriateness of the moment, and assess the facts and possibly suggestions before engaging with the boss. It is never a good idea to correct or confront the boss in front of others. That is confrontational and not good for boss-subordinate relations.

Generally a gentleman takes control of the boss-subordinate relationship, emotionally intelligent and optimistically prepared to make the best of the relationship. Bad bosses have their good days and good sides which must make a difference. Bad experiences are also learning experiences.

A perfect gentleman is one that makes the best opportunity to work with any boss at all and never tries to outshine the boss.

"Your work is going to fill a large part of your life, and the only way to be truly satisfied is to do what you believe is great work. And the only way to do great work is to love what you do."
~ Steve Jobs

RULE #46

Teams and Projects

"Talent wins games, but teamwork and intelligence win championships."
~ Michael Jordan

....

A perfect gentleman is bound to work in a team or with teams at some point. A team is any group of people organized to work together, both independently and cooperatively to accomplish a common goal or purpose.

A perfect gentleman ensures that he makes a difference wherever he finds himself including working in a team. Teams work in sync towards a specific goal. These goals may be project based. A project is a set of tasks that have a definite beginning and end and are set to bring out creativity, resilience and excellence in a person. Every project is a test of competence which must be overcome by a gentleman. Various aspects of life present themselves in the form of projects; schooling, finding a life partner, building or purchasing a first house, building a home and family, building a career etc.

A perfect gentleman handles life and indeed, every aspect of life as a project, knowing that life does not last forever.

"Arriving at one goal is the starting point to another."
~ John Dewey

RULE #47

Workplace Romance:

"If you don't behave properly, an office romance can cause conflict and have a negative impact on your career".
~Barbara Pachter

....

It is okay to fall in love. But it is certainly not okay to fall in love in the wrong place, at the wrong time and with the wrong person. Falling in love at the workplace is one of those tricky situations.

First is that it should be authorised. Some workplaces do not allow for relationships with colleague workers and so that may be the starting point for a gentleman. The workplace is not a place to play hide and seek in the name of love if it is not allowed. Assuming however that it is allowed, should it be encouraged?

There are legal issues to this. No problems occur while a workplace relationship goes on smoothly. But when they hit the snag, with a little disagreement here, or a bit of jealousy there, it often becomes a problem. An aggrieved lady may claim and file sexual harassment complaints and create confusion in the workplace. The gentleman on occasion may become a target for other males especially more senior males if they are also interested in the same lady.

For a perfect gentleman, workplace romance cannot be encouraged for it is the wrong place to pursue the right agenda. Workplace is for work and anything that becomes a distraction must be discouraged.

A perfect gentleman should therefore be aware of the workplace policies that regulate workplace romance. Where it is absolutely safe and most allowed by policy, a gentleman may explore the opportunities of love in the workplace, though not encouraged.

A perfect gentleman must be open and honest about his feelings when dealing with a lady in the workplace or any lady at all for that matter. Its is essential to make your immediate supervisor aware or a senior officer aware of your workplace relationship as a buffer and guide should things begin to go wrong.

"My only relationship policy is, don't bring your dirty laundry to work, no sex on company furniture and don't let it affect your work."
~ Paula Graves

RULE #48

Rewards and Promotion

"The way to get started is to quit talking and begin doing."
~Walt Disney

....

Vrooms Expectancy Theory of motivation states that a person is motivated to act in anticipation of an expected reward. People will act more purposefully when assured that their expectations will be met.

It is only human nature to desire growth, and a gentleman should strive to grow in his career and dominate the workplace.

Knowing the criteria required for reward in an organization is key, especially regarding performance expectations, conduct and behaviour.

A perfect gentleman must endeavour to be in good standing with regard to reward criteria in order to attain deserved rewards.

For every reward offered, a gentleman must be grateful, accreting what comes and being aware that reward is always discretionary and not mandatory. A reward is a gift of appreciation conferred upon and resulting from high recognition.

For every reward obtained, another person loses out and hence a gentleman must be magnanimous, appreciative, grateful and not excessively rub it in the face of others.

Carry out a random act of kindness, with no expectation of reward, safe in the knowledge that one day someone might do the same for you.
~ Princess Diana

RULE #49

Travels on Official Business

"If you can't fly then run, if you can't run then walk, if you can't walk then crawl, but whatever you do you have to keep moving forward."
~ Dr. Martin Luther King, Jr.

....

Travel on official Business is inevitable in the life of a gentleman. In fact they will occur in droves, sometimes for long periods on end. What does a business trip entail and what must a gentleman look out for?

What to pack: What to pack depends on how much time the trip is expected to last. Where the trip will take more than a week (5 days), pack items to last for two weeks as clothes can be recycled for reuse in the third and subsequent weeks. Travel packs can be classified into three categories; Toiletries (Grooming items including first aid and other medication), Clothes (including footwear and clothes for exercise and leisure) and Work Tools and Equipment (Phone, Electronic Pads, Laptops,

Reference Material and other work related equipment).
As much as possible, a gentleman is expected to travel
light with a minimum luggage as possible. A gentleman
always ensures however that there is enough baggage
allowance for shopping items for self and a gift or two
for loved ones when returning from the trip.

Travel Itinerary: Travel itinerary and other travel
documents should be kept in a separate space and easy
to reach. Bus/Train/Air boarding tickets with passports
or other personal identification documents must be
kept in close proximity for inspection.

What to eat: A plausible advise I have always followed
is that where in doubt about what to eat on a trip, look
for and order Chinese food. Everyone loves Chinese
food and Chinese food is found in most places on
all continents. Beyond this, undertake a bit of food
exploration on the first few days of your arrival to settle
on foods that sit well with your palate and tummy.
A gentleman always keeps medication for 'running
tummy' as part of first aid kit.

What to wear: Ordinarily, clothing on business trips
are supposed to be official work clothes. But for the
comfort of packing and convenience of preparing
clothing before wearing, it is suggested that a gentleman
carefully chooses work clothes that are easiest to prepare
and possibly needs no ironing before wearing. That

makes it easy to handle clothes on the trip as well as maximise time for preparing clothes before wearing as ironing and laundary services often come at cost.

A gentleman must prepare at least one official clothing for dinners or formal events. Other clothes should be smart casual as well as a sleep wear.

Where to go: Business trips can be boring and hence requires some exploration, looking around and visiting popular places near the town of lodging. Entertainment is also a necessity. Hence a gentleman should investigate carefully which safe entertainment options are available to pursue. Often, hosts would assist with entertainment options depending on what is available.

"If you think adventure is dangerous, try routine; it's lethal."
~ Paulo Coelho

RULE #50

Resolving Grievances

You can't hold on to a grievance and be happy. Time to make a choice!
~ Robert Holden

....

Disputes and disagreements are inevitable. They will always occur. Encountering them is a surety but effectively dealing with them is the most headache.

People face several disagreements with others. But a gentleman is one who maturely and diplomatically comes out of a dispute situation unscathed.

The good book says, "Settle matters quickly with your adversary who is taking you to court. Do it while you are still together on the way. Or your adversary may hand you over to the judge, and the judge may hand you over to the officer, and you may be thrown into prison. (Mathew 5:25, The Holy Bible)

Every effort must be made to settle disputes and grievances quickly. Following steps may help.

Step 1: Understand what the issue is.

Step 2: Examine the reason why it is an issue and what the stakes are.

Step 3: Think through various mediums through which you may have them resolved.

Step 4: Engage the other person against whom you have the grievance and talk it out long enough to reach an agreeable resolution.

Step 5: If this is not possible, engage through a reliable third party neutral person.

Step 6: If steps 4 & 5 fail, revert to Step 3 and change the medium of engagement.

CONCLUSION

When all is said and done, a man is what he thinks, what he does and what he truly feels and perceives.

No one achieved great things by worrying about what others think. The true application of wisdom is listening to others and applying a personal opinion that stems from past knowledge, beliefs and the circumstances of the moment, to the benefit of self and others.

This book is a necessary guide to boys and men as it enables them to learn about how to strive towards becoming perfect gentlemen. On the contrary, though there is no such thing as a perfect gentleman, the book offers an opportunity for boys and men to discover their unique personal styles and 'chi.'

The world of work and business require winners with confidence and style. The world is in need of perfect gentlemen with fine rounded personalities who are also able to exhibit exceptional social and intellectual skills in their various fields of expertise.

I do hope that each reader has found in this book an excellent guide to renewed personality, confidence and purpose.

EPILOGUE

RULE #51

"Finally brethren, whatsoever things are true, whatsoever things are honest, whatsoever things are just, whatsoever things are pure, whatsoever things are lovely, whatsoever things are of good report; if there be virtue, and if there be any praise, think on these things."

~ Apostle Paul's Letter to the Philippians 4:8 (The Holy Bible - KJV)

....

...for A Perfect Gentleman